Ornamental Painted Boxes

Ornamental Painted Boxes

How to decorate boxes beautifully

Hertha Wascher

THORSONS PUBLISHING GROUP

First UK Edition published 1989

First published by Rosenheimer Verlagshaus Alfred Forg GmbH & Co.,
8200 Rosenheim, Germany

British Library Cataloguing in Publication Data

Wascher, Hertha
Ornamental painted boxes: how to decorate
boxes beautifully.
1. Decorative boxes. Making
I. Title
745.594

ISBN 0-7225-1814-5

Translated by Janet Winslow

Craft editor Eileen Lowcock

Plates 1–4 from the National Museum of Germany, Nuremberg, plate 24
from Rudolf Moser, Upper Austria, remaining plates from Wilfried
Wascher. Cover photograph by Wilfried Wascher

Patterns drawn by Hedwig Wascher, except those on pages 91–95 which
appear courtesy of Dover Publications Inc. from *American Folk Art
Designs and Motifs for Artists and Craftsmen* by Joseph D'Addetta, Dover
Pictorial Archive Series, 1984

*Published by Thorsons Publishers Limited,
Wellingborough, Northamptonshire, NN8 2RQ, England*

Printed in Italy by G. Canale & C. S.p.A. - Turin

1 3 5 7 9 10 8 6 4 2

Contents

Introduction

Beautifully decorated boxes have always been a pleasure to own or to give as gifts. They can store all manner of precious, favourite things attractively or sit, empty, and be purely eye-catching ornaments.

Craft shops and galleries sell beautiful painted and decorated boxes, imported from countries all over the world – for a price, even though the boxes themselves are inexpensive. It is the *decoration* that adds the value and appeal, and antique decorated boxes are valued collectors' items.

The methods of decoration are, however, simple – they can be grasped by anyone who is prepared to pick up a paintbrush. Decorating boxes is also very absorbing and great fun.

There are, of course, intricate and complex designs that will challenge the really artistic amongst us, but most of the designs are based on folk art patterns motifs and are stunningly simple to do. If you can make patterns just doodling with a pencil, then painting boxes will be merely taking your doodles one step further, using a paintbrush rather than a pencil *and* you'll have a lovely box too!

The art of decorating boxes for storing all sorts of personal and house-hold items flourished throughout Europe and America during the eight-eenth and nineteenth centuries. The best of traditional designs from that period are collected together in this book and were found in museums or private collections in Austria, Bavaria and Germany. There are also some American designs for a truly international flavour.

The history of painted boxes

Originally, ornamental painted boxes were purely functional objects, in daily use. It is only in this century that they have been raised to the status of collectors' pieces and become essential accessories for well decorated rooms.

It is not possible to determine when these boxes were first produced, but it is certain that their popularity was at its height throughout Europe and America during the eighteenth and nineteenth centuries. At this time there may well have been woodworkers co-operatives in most of the pine-forested regions of Europe. As a rule the craftsmen who made these boxes also produced other practical articles and wooden toys. It is certain however, that boxes were produced before then on a smaller scale. The oldest box found so far dates from 1478.

Smaller boxes were made first and the larger boxes are the cheaper descendants of the small hardwood and metal chests and caskets that enjoyed wide and varying use in the Middle Ages. The boxes not only held documents, testimonies, jewellery and valuables, but also items that were used repeatedly in farming families, such as christening gowns and wedding finery. The boxes were particularly important for storing headdresses from traditional costumes and hats and bonnets of all kinds. Probably most of the boxes that were used every day were not decorated because, even at that time, the painted versions were expensive.

The small boxes came in a wide variety of designs and were used for many different purposes. For instance, chemists and veterinary surgeons used them to dispense their medicines, and in the army, they were issued to the soldiers along with cloths for shoe cleaning equipment. These boxes were unpainted, although, for special products, the manufacturer's label would be stuck on the top of the box (see plate 7).

Boxes filled with sweets and other treats at fairs were usually coloured with a red stain and sometimes the lid was also decorated with a printed floral design. The smallest of these boxes were stained red and exported from Austria to Turkey where they were used as containers for selling make-up.

Traditional production techniques

Only wood that could be split into thin strips with a special axe was used in the manufacture of the boxes. Almost every tree can be sawn into planks but not every tree lends itself to splitting. It must have grown as straight as possible and have evenly spaced growth rings. Only a tree grown in a sunny position, protected from the wind, has these characteristics.

Spruce is the most suitable, although pine was also used. Willow was favoured, too, because of its flexibility, for the narrow strips of wood that bound the box sides together and, indeed, for the sides themselves as they could be shaped more easily. Rowan was also used for the same reason and sometimes just the bark of these trees was used.

Large boxes
The height of the sides of a box was limited by the thickness of the tree trunk. There are hardly any boxes higher than 16–17 cm. If higher sides were required, as in the case of hat boxes, two strips of wood were placed one on top of the other and a narrow strip of wood was glued along the join.

The thin, planed strips that were used to make a box were first made smooth with a knife, then placed for some time in cold water and then briefly in hot. Both ends were then bent around a box-shaped wooden block and clamped into position.

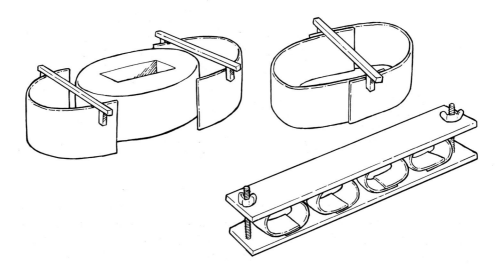

The clamps were removed only when the wood was completely dry and then the sides were glued together. A special knife was used to make small slits in the glued join and, through these slits, narrow strips of willow or rowan were threaded. In some areas these strips were dyed red before they were used. The method of drawing strips of wood through slits in the box sides varied greatly depending on where they were manufactured.

After the sides had been glued and threaded together, a base was cut out. In old boxes a thicker strip of wood was used and occasionally the pencil line that was drawn onto the wood as a guide for the cutting out can still be seen on the inside of the base.

Small boxes
Manufacturers of small boxes were less exacting in their choice of wood and they sometimes used lesser quality spruce or even pine.

For small boxes, produced on a commercial basis, the sides were cut using a plane. A block of wood was sawn to the dimensions of the box, then planed into strips. The plane used in the process resembled a large cucumber slicer. The lid and base of these boxes were cut out using metal stamps and a wooden mallet, as you can see below.

As for the large boxes, the planed sides were first stuck together into hoops, and then the lid and base were glued into place. To ensure that it didn't fall off when the box was closed, the lid could be bigger than the sides by no more than the thickness of the sides.

As the boxes in Europe were produced primarily for export, they were made in co-ordinating sizes so that they could be placed inside each other, which made them easier to transport. This range of sizes was known as a set and a set consisted of 6 to 12 boxes (see colour plate 26). The manufacturer therefore had to work with more or less standard models and, in addition, use clamps that were exactly the right size. That may be the reason why the dimensions of these boxes have remained practically unaltered for almost 200 years.

How to paint boxes in the traditional way

The boxes

Plain wooden boxes that are just right for painting are available from larger craft suppliers and from mail-order companies specializing in craft materials. They come in a wide variety of shapes and sizes, including round, oval and rectangular, and with or without hinges and fastenings. It is easier to start by working on small boxes and work up to larger ones as you have less surface area to cover.

The base coat

The painting of the boxes begins with the base coat. This stage is important because the success of the overall decoration depends on it. There are two different types of base coat: transparent or opaque.

Transparent base coats are clear washes that colour the surface but, at the same time, allow the texture of the wood to show through. These are known as stains. They contain no binding agent and dye the cellulose of the wood. If you do not want to use wood stain you can paint your boxes with dyes recommended for cotton fabrics to achieve the same effect.

Most of the early boxes were stained red, but darker colours, such as green and blue, have become popular in more recent times because dark colours really make the painted designs stand out well.

Opaque colours allow the texture of the wood to show through only slightly, if at all. They consist of a binding agent into which the paint powder is stirred. Household emulsion paints make an ideal base coat, as do Pelikan Plaka paints which are available in a large range of colours.

If you choose to use an opaque base coat, you must use a wood primer first to seal the wood. If you use Plaka paints, then use Plaka painting medium as a primer.

When you put on the base coat, use the paint as sparingly as possible and apply it with a fairly large brush, working in the direction of the wood grain. Clean the brush when you've finished. It is a good idea to leave the inside and bottom of the box unpainted. Not only is this traditional, but it shows off the character of the wood you are decorating.

It is essential to have a perfectly smooth surface to paint on so, when the paint or stain has dried, rub it down with very fine sandpaper until it is smooth. Then just give it a dust with a soft cloth. It is a good idea to have a testing board on which you can try a colour out. This is particularly useful when you are working on a large box.

Drawing the pattern

Once the surface of the box has been well prepared, draw on the pattern, lightly, using a white crayon or piece of chalk that can be wiped off easily when you have finished the painting. As the painting is done freehand, the drawing consists only of guidelines that divide up the space.

Determine the size of the central design with one line, then leave a gap and draw a second line to indicate the extent of the edging decoration. It is also important to mark the central point with a cross. Indicate the individual motifs, such as flowers or hearts with a circle. Then apply fine brush strokes freehand to fill in the pattern.

The decoration on most boxes consists of a central motif, a space, then an enclosing band of colour or a narrow border design. The success or otherwise of the finished box depends on how well you use the space.

Paints

The colours used should all be of the same make. You cannot mix different makes of paint. If you do, the paint cracks after drying and peels off. Although all types of paint can be used, as you can see with the American-style decorations, we suggest you try Pelikan Plaka paints. These are tempera colours and can be diluted with water when working on an opaque base colour. They can be used on their own or, for greater adhesion and elasticity, mixed with Plaka painting medium. Pelikan Plaka Plus acrylic paints can be used directly onto the wood without a primer or over a stained base coat.

Old boxes were painted using very few colours. Mostly only four colours were used, two of which often made up the base. White does not count as a colour. Sharp contrasts of colour can be avoided by painting one colour over another – a pink over white, for example, or red over yellow. The art of painting boxes lies not in the type of paint used, since most commercial products are suitable, but in the mixing together of the right co-ordinating colours.

Colour mixing

Do not use the paints directly from the tube or pot. There is no shade of yellow or green that can be used without it first being toned down. The most difficult shade to achieve is the bluey/green found on some of the very old boxes. Here, only practice and a feeling for colour will help.

Practise by trying out colours on paper. The colour is altered by gradually adding small amounts of another colour. Make a note of the colour ratios for future reference and, once you have decided upon a shade, mix enough paint to complete the project. Store the mixed paint in an air-tight container if you have to stop in the middle of painting your box. (Once water has been mixed with paint, it will not keep for long, so use it fairly quickly.)

When the paint is dry, you can apply further colours. The details in white are the last to be added. Bear in mind too that the colours will darken when the final protective coat of clear matt or gloss varnish is applied.

Brushes

It is advisable to buy a selection of good quality artists' brushes for painting. Sizes 2 to 6 are the most useful. Test the brushes in the shop to ensure they come to a good point when wet. You need a larger brush for the base coat and this can be cheaper, but make sure it does not shed its bristles!

As soon as you have finished using a brush, wash it out in warm, soapy water. Do not leave a brush standing in water or it will bend and you will not be able to use it again.

Painting a box in the traditional style
Materials
- a small, round or oval box
- wood stain or Pelikan painting medium or wood primer and paint
- paint brushes
- fine sandpaper
- Pelikan Plaka or Plaka Plus paints
- white crayon
- clear varnish

What to do
If you are going to use an opaque base coat, use a fairly large brush to paint the outside of the box and lid with wood primer or Plaka painting medium, leaving the inside and base of the box plain. Otherwise, paint on a base coat of wood stain. When the base coat is completely dry, sandpaper gently with fine sandpaper until the surface is smooth.

Select a simple design to start with, such as those shown on pages 38 and 39. Divide the surface of the box into the main areas of the design and mark these lightly with crayon. For example, the top left design on page 38 has three main areas. Then, mark the positions of the main motifs with a circle or a dot.

Using finely pointed brushes, paint the design freehand onto the box.

Wipe off any remaining crayon marks before giving the box a coat of clear matt or gloss varnish.

American milk painting

In America during the eighteenth and nineteenth centuries, Pennsylvanian Germans and immigrants from many parts of Europe all decorated wooden cupboards, tables, chairs, chests and boxes with colourful hand-painted designs. The designs consisted of hearts, flowers, animals, hex symbols and abstract figures. These decorations were usually painted by the man of the house or by local craftsmen and the designs were simple and uncomplicated. The paints they used consisted of natural pigments such as blood, clay, earth and juices from berries and plants mixed to a creamy consistency with skimmed milk.

Materials for the paint
- skimmed powdered milk
- warm water
- wooden spoon
- natural pigments, acrylic paints or inks

What to do
Place some powdered milk in a bowl and slowly add some warm water, stirring all the time with a wooden spoon, mixing to a thick, creamy consistency.

Add pigment or other colouring, such as acrylic paint or ink to colour the mixture. The paint is now ready to use.

The paint will dry to an attractive matt finish in twelve hours and, once dry, the decoration should last for over 100 years! Articles decorated with milk paints have a strange smell which will gradually fade away. If you do not like this smell, simply seal the paint with a coat of varnish.

Materials for milk painted boxes
- a small wooden box
- fine sandpaper
- milk paints

- artists' paint brushes
- paper
- soft- and hard-leaded pencils
- tracing paper
- a pair of compasses

What to do

Prepare the surface of the box by smoothing it down with sandpaper. Give the box a thorough wipe with a soft cloth to clean away the dust from sanding as this can spoil the look of the finished box.

Choose a colour for the base coat of the box. Mix the paint well and brush on a single coat, working in the direction of the wood grain. The grain should show through the paint and contribute an interesting textural effect to the decoration.

While the base coat is drying, plan a design on paper to fit the area to be filled. (Hexes can be drawn using a pair of compasses.)

Using a soft-leaded pencil, draw the design onto tracing paper. Bear in mind that the design will be reversed when it appears on the box. When the base coat is completely dry, place the tracing paper pencil-side down onto the box, taking care to align edge patterns with the edges of the box and hold it in place with masking tape, then, carefully trace the pattern with a hard-leaded pencil, using medium pressure. When you have traced the whole pattern, lift the tracing paper off the box and you should find that you have transferred the soft-pencilled design onto your box. If there are places where the design is faint, just complete it with the soft-leaded pencil.

Using a small range of good strong colours, paint the main design shapes. Then pick out the dot details to complete the design.

American-style painted boxes

These differ from the traditional milk painted designs in that primary and bright, clear colours are used. Also black is generally used to highlight the designs instead of white.

Materials
- a wooden box
- a selection of artists' brushes
- tracing paper
- pencil
- masking tape

- Plaka Plus paints
- clear matt or gloss varnish

What to do

Choose a primary colour for the base coat and apply one coat.

Taking a tracing of your chosen design and, using the same method given on page 14 for milk painted boxes, transfer the design through to the box.

Fill in the design with a soft-leaded pencil if parts have not transferred too well.

Using primary and clear, bright colours, paint the design.

When the paint is completely dry, use a very finely pointed brush and black paint to work over the lines of the design and pick out the dot and dash details.

A simplified method

Almost any colouring medium can be used to decorate boxes. It is worth experimenting with new and modern materials to see what effects may be achieved but always test them first on a piece of scrap wood rather than on the box you wish to decorate.

Materials

- a small box
- paper
- fine sandpaper
- soft- and hard-leaded pencils
- tracing paper
- felt-tipped pens or Plaka Pen paint markers
- clear matt or gloss varnish
- paint brush

What to do

Prepare the surface of the box for decoration by smoothing it with fine sandpaper.

Select a simple design and draw this onto tracing paper using a soft-leaded pencil then transfer it onto the box using the method described on page 14. Draw over any faint lines with a soft-leaded pencil to make them clear.

Using felt-tipped pens, colour in the design. To protect and enhance the box, give it a coat of clear matt or gloss varnish.

Lining boxes

Old American boxes were often lined with newspaper and, if you want to give your box a traditional finish you can do the same.

Simply cut out shapes for the base and the lid and a strip for the sides of the box, allowing an overlap on one side and one end.

Along the side, snip into the overlap at regular intervals. Then, spread glue over the back of all three pieces of newspaper.

Stick the lining for the sides into the box so that the slashed overlap rests on the base of the box where it will be covered by the lining for the base. To finish, stick in place the lining for the base and the lid. Really press down the edges of the paper.

For a prettier finish you can use gift-wrap paper to compliment the design on the outside of the box or paper in a plain colour or marbled paper. You can, of course, leave the inside plain or line it with fabric or felt in the same way as described for paper. Use firmly woven, non-fray fabrics for the best effect and use a latex fabric adhesive to stick it in place.

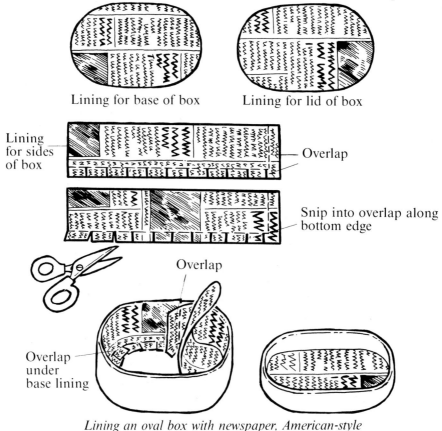

Lining for base of box Lining for lid of box

Lining for sides of box — Overlap

Snip into overlap along bottom edge

Overlap

Overlap under base lining

Lining an oval box with newspaper, American-style

16

A particularly attractive ornamental box displaying a very popular pattern. It appears over and over again in many variations.

2 and 3   *Typical German ornamental boxes.*

4   *A very rare box. The unusually perfect painting could only have been carried out by a master painter.*

5   *In the illustration on page 34, the pattern on this box is adapted for a heart-shaped box.*

6   *This box has divisions inside. The design for this round box is adapted for a square box with rounded corners on page 35.*

7   These boxes were made and decorated at the turn of the century except the small, oval box and the triangular box which are originals. Patterns are on pages 36–38.

8   This box was made in 1796. You can find the patterns for it on pages 40–41.

9   This antique box shows particularly refined painting on its lid. The reduced pattern is shown on page 39.

10 *An antique box. You can find the design enlarged on page 42.*

11 *Only the sides have survived of the two lower boxes. The patterns for these are on page 43.*

12 *This splendid large box was found in Austria.*

21

13 *An antique box displaying typical patterns. The design on the lid can be found on pages 44–45.*

14 *This large, flat antique box was used to hold a crucifix. The pattern for this is shown on page 46.*

15 *A selection of ornamental boxes. The designs for two of the boxes shown are on pages 47–49.*

16 and 17 *This tall, slender box (diameter 30 cm, height 30 cm) was probably used to contain fur caps. The designs are on pages 50–51.*

18 *This tall box is made from two planed pieces of wood set one on top of the other and was probably used to store hats.*

19 *A box with absolutely classic designs. The designs are on page 52.*

20 *This large box is made in the traditional way. The lid design is illustrated on page 53.*

21 *The two boxes shown here are family heirlooms.*

22 *This is a particularly splendidly painted box. The designs are on page 54.*

24

3　*A modest but tastefully painted box. Note the unusual brown base coat. For the design, see pages 56–57.*

24   *This box has a particularly naturalistic flower pattern and dates from about 1870.*

25   *The boxes and caskets shown here are all painted in the same style. The pattern, drawn on pages 58–59, was very popular and numerous examples still exist.*

26

26 *This complete set of 10 boxes from the second half of the nineteenth century was discovered, unopened, in the attic of a castle. The original colours have therefore been preserved.*

27 *The decorations on these boxes include religious motifs. For the patterns, see pages 60–61.*

28 *The Holy Family is represented beautifully and simply on the lid of this box in medallions.*

28

29   *This box was used to store sacred objects such as a monstrance.*

30   *These are original, antique boxes. The right-hand box shows Joseph set in a flower on the lid. See pages 63–65 for the design.*

31 *A set of ornamental boxes showing different designs, but in all cases they are very true to the old originals. Patterns relating to these are to be found on pages 66–67.*

32 *The original painting of the sides of the left-hand box, showing house fronts, is particularly unusual. The designs are on pages 68–70.*

This box shows a typical but delicately worked design.

34   It is not known where this box originated from. Only the sides are original – the lid is reconstructed. For the patterns, see pages 72–73.

35   Here are three different, recently made and decorated boxes based on old patterns. See the illustrations on pages 74–77. There are also suggestions for patterns for decorating the sides of the boxes.

36   The very old box on the right has a lock and hinges and was almost certainly used to store valuables. For the pattern see page 78.

Traditional motif for an oval box with a reddish-brown background

33

Pattern from page 5, adapted so that you can use it on a different shaped box

Pattern from plate 6

35

Pattern from plate 7

Pattern from plate 7

Pattern from plate 7

Pattern from plate 9

39

Pattern from plate 8

Pattern from plate 8

Pattern from plate 10

42

Pattern from plate 11

Pattern from plate 13 (on the original box, the dots were picked out in gold leaf. You can use gold paint instead if you wish, as you can on all the designs if you want to)

44

Pattern from plate 13

45

Pattern from plate 14

46

Pattern from plate 15

47

Pattern from plate 15

48

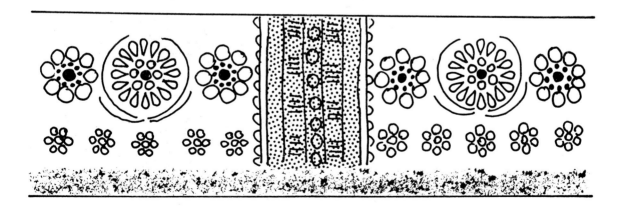

Pattern from plate 15

49

Pattern from plates 16 and 17

50

Pattern from plates 16 and 17

Pattern from plate 19

52

Pattern from plate 20

Pattern from plate 22

54

Modern flower motif based on traditional patterns – white foliage and pink flowers on a ruby-coloured background

Pattern from plate 23

Pattern from plate 23

Pattern from plate 25

Pattern from plate 25

59

Pattern from plate 27 for a squarer box

Suggestions for patterns for the sides of your box

61

Modern motif based on traditional patterns – red or blue flowers on a green or red background, set amongst white or yellow foliage

Pattern from plate 30 for a squarer box

63

Pattern from plate 30

Pattern from plate 30

Pattern from plate 31

Pattern from plate 31

67

Pattern from plate 32

68

Pattern from plate 32

69

Pattern from plate 32

Modern lid design based on a traditional pattern (on the original box, the dotted areas were worked in gold leaf but you can use gold paint if you wish)

Pattern from plate 34

72

Pattern from plate 34

73

Pattern from plate 35

74

Pattern from plate 35

75

Patterns from plate 35

Patterns from plate 35

Pattern from plate 36

Modern motif of red tulips on a green background (this relatively simple design is particularly suitable if you are a beginner)

Pattern from the cover

Patterns from the cover

81

Pattern from the cover

Patterns from the cover

Patterns from the cover

84

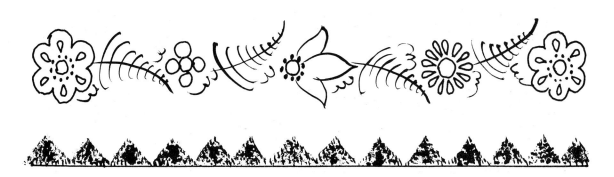

Patterns from the cover

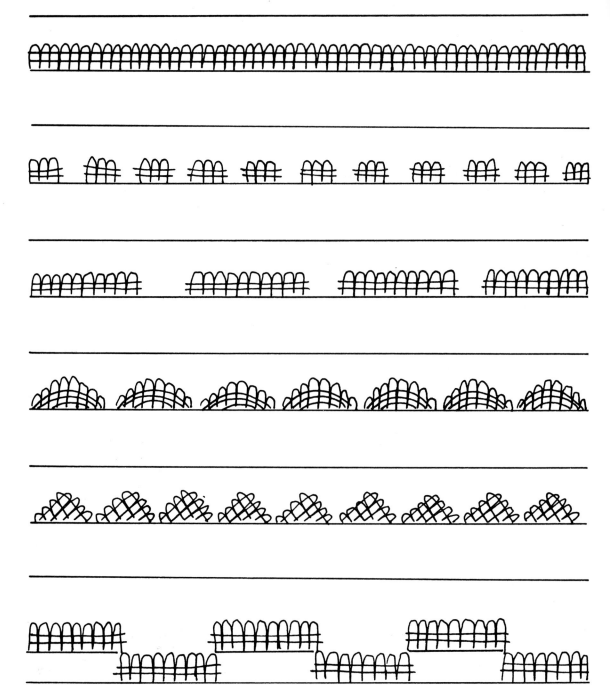

These two pages show different options for traditional white edging patterns – the fuzzy edged ones are painted or printed with a sponge

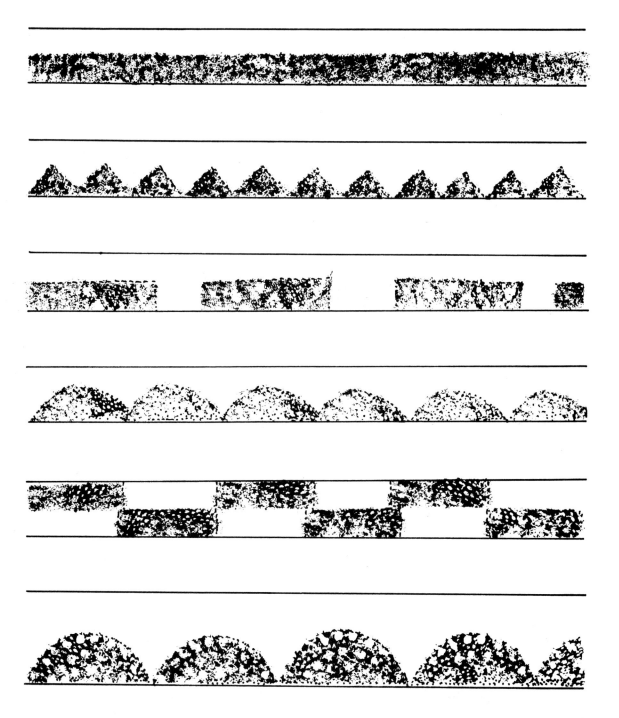

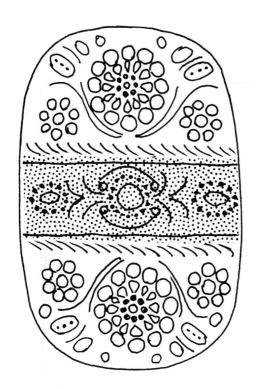 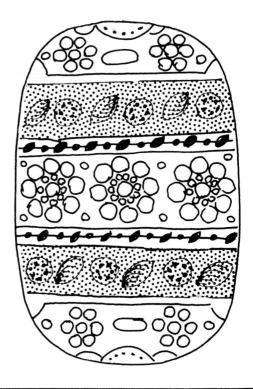

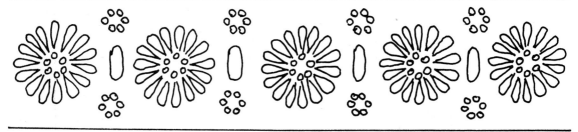

These two pages show traditional motifs for smaller boxes, the flowers mainly being painted in bright colours on a ruby or brown background

Traditional patterns for smaller boxes, mainly featuring brightly coloured flowers on a brown or ruby background

A typical hex design

A pattern that was used as a stencil in Pennsylvania in 1825

Floral motifs from 1820   *A tulip motif from a painted chest dating from 1710*

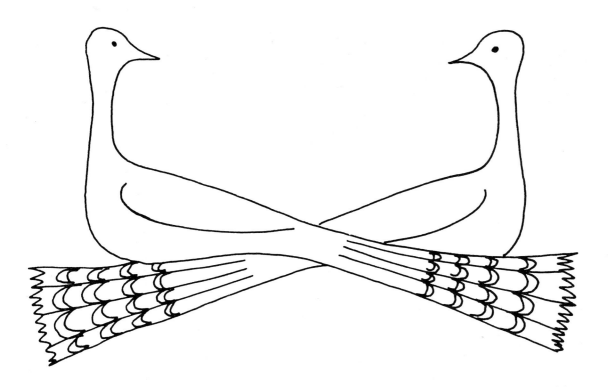

Pair of birds motif painted in Massachusetts about 1800

Border patterns from a painted wooden box made in Pennsylvania in 1840

Floral motif from a painted chest made in Connecticut in 1790

Border motif used on a wooden box made in 1810